Organizing

FOR
DUMMIES®

POCKET EDITION

**by Eileen Roth
with Elizabeth Miles**

Wiley Publishing, Inc.

Organizing For Dummies,® Pocket Edition

Published by
Wiley Publishing, Inc.
111 River Street
Hoboken, NJ 07030-5774
www.wiley.com

Copyright © 2007 by Wiley Publishing, Inc., Indianapolis, Indiana

Published by Wiley Publishing, Inc., Indianapolis, Indiana

Published simultaneously in Canada

Table of Contents

Introduction

● ●

*W*hat's the favorite four-letter word of less-than-fully organized people? "Help!" Answering that call has given me a satisfying career and my 15 minutes on the *Today* show and *Oprah*. In case you missed the shows or absorbing life-changing information takes you more than 15 minutes, I'm here to answer the call for you with *Organizing For Dummies,* Pocket Edition.

If you think of yourself as an organizational dummy, don't feel bad; everybody is born that way. Organization isn't inherited. With the human genome decoded, the evidence is clear: DNA strings dedicated to putting things into place and managing your time like a pro are nonexistent. Instead, organization is a learned skill set, just like driving a car. In fact that's a pretty good analogy. If you think back, learning to drive probably seemed pretty daunting at first, but driving may now be so automatic that you can practically drive in your sleep (though national safety experts don't recommend this). Organization is acquired, and as in any learning process, you need help. This book offers you that help.

Icons Used in This Book

I direct your attention to all sorts of helpful hints for getting organized in *Organizing For Dummies,* Pocket Edition, with a system of icons that help you scan right to the juicy stuff on any given page. Here's an overview of what you'll see.

Extra ideas to aid the points made.

This warns you of possible problems.

Points to remember that will save you time and trouble later.

Cut-to-the-chase ways to clean up that mess.

Where to Go from Here

You've got your minibook copy of *Organizing For Dummies,* Pocket Edition — now what? This minibook is a reference, so if you're already in the middle of a project and just need some help deciding how to finish it, think about reading Chapter 2 first — it's meant just for you and includes a lot of pointers on choosing the right containers and properly labeling. If you're wanting to hone your organizational skills, skip on over to Chapter 3. Or heck, start with Chapter 1 and read the chapters in order . . . you rebel. If you want even more advice on organizing, from specific strategies for your bathroom to tackling that office, check out the full-size version of *Organizing For Dummies* — simply head to your local book seller or go to www.dummies.com!

Chapter 1

Training Your Mind to Be Organized

● ●

In This Chapter

▶ Organization as a state of mind

▶ Setting your organizing goals

▶ Making time to get organized

▶ Breaking down jobs into bite-size pieces

▶ Personalizing your organizing plan

▶ Maintaining an easy mindset to end yo-yo organizing

● ●

*O*rganization isn't inherited — organizing is learned. That means that whatever disorganized secrets lurk in your past or what a mess you see when you assess your present condition, you can become organized and stay that way for a lifetime.

"But organizing sounds hard!" you may think, and that could be the case if I were talking about calculus and you'd only gone as far as basic algebra. But I'm not. Though there are many useful principles and tips behind getting organized in every aspect of your life — a whole book's worth in fact — thinking like an organized person isn't rocket science. Being organized is simply a habit, just like brushing your teeth, which, believe it or not, you once didn't know how to do.

Organization begins in the mind. Once you've got those synaptic connections in place, you can start to see what to do even before I tell you. Take a few minutes to read this chapter to get a jump-start on the organizational mindset, as well as how to organize the process of getting organized. After all, how can you get started if there's a mess in your mind?

Your Organizing Plan

The first step in wrapping your mind around the organizational challenge is to make a plan. How to begin? What next? Start with a basic planning tool that will pop up throughout the book. To make a plan, simply think like a journalist. No, not "man bites dog." This technique is what I call the Five Ws Plus How — six questions reporters ask when writing a story, and that can put any plan into place: Who? What? When? Where? Why? How? These are easy questions, but actively answering them can help you make a concrete plan.

Organizing your mission

Why do you want to get organized? To create an organized mindset, you need a mission. Saving time, saving money, reducing stress, enhancing performance, building self-esteem, and improving relationships may figure into your organizing mission. For me it always boils down to my trademark phrase, which you just read a few paragraphs back: Get organized to enjoy life.™

Aren't those little trademark signs nifty? By the way, you definitely need to be organized if you ever want to deal with the Office of Trademarks and Patents. But that's a story for another day.

Take a minute now to decide on your organizing mission statement. Here are a few examples:

- My mission is to get organized so that I can enjoy more time with my family and friends.

- I want to improve my organizing skills to achieve my true potential at work.

- Our group's objective is to use organizational techniques to speed processes, facilitate communications, and reduce individual stress levels.

Have you got your mission statement? Good. Write it down here.

_____

_____

_____

_____

_____

Your organizing goals

What are your organizing goals? Once you've got a mission, you can set specific objectives. Do you want to organize your home? Your office? Your time? One after the other in priority order? The point is not to try to take on everything at once, but to focus on what you want to do now. You can select a single closet or an officewide process. You might want to shape up your computer files or finally find the right containers for your kids' toys. Maybe the main immediate goal is to clean up your living room so you can welcome friends and family into your home. You may have one goal or ten, big ones or small ones. Perhaps your goals have a domino effect — if you get one done, then you want to do another. Can you guess what I'd like you to do with your organizing goals? That's right — write them down.

_____

_____

_____

_____

_____

_____

_____

_____

Your organizing time

When's a good time to get organized? Eventually, the answer may be "all the time," but when you're just getting started, being more specific helps. Spring cleaning, fall cleanup, the new year, or start of the school year are all natural times to get organized. A big deadline at work may spur you to organize at the office. Knowing the family is coming for Thanksgiving can get you in gear at home. Moving? You better get organized from bottom to top.

One of the most frequent complaints I hear is, "I don't have time to get organized!" Have you ever made such an assertion yourself? The less time you have, the more you stand to benefit from organization, so break down the time barrier with five easy techniques for managing your organizing time.

Chunking your chores

Looking at the whole picture of what you need to organize can be so overwhelming that you don't get started at all. Or maybe you do, but then you quit in an hour because there's still so much left to do. Biting off more than you can chew isn't comfortable in your mouth or your mind — so chunk it instead.

When you don't have the time or concentration to complete the whole Herculean job, simply break up tasks into bite-size pieces that you can reasonably accomplish. Choose one file drawer at a time, and soon you can have the whole filing system down. Start with a single kitchen cabinet and do the second one tomorrow or next week. Rome wasn't built in a day. Chunk what you want to do and get underway.

Setting a time limit

The kitchen timer lets you know when something is done cooking. Use it to signal when you're done organizing too. When you set a time limit, things get done. You know there's a deadline, and you may even find yourself racing the clock to accomplish as much as you can before it rings. If you think you have about an hour to work, take a timer, whether your watch or a clock or the one you use while you cook, and set it for your stop time. There's a trick to this: Subtract 10 minutes from the time you want to work — for instance, an hour becomes 50 minutes — so you have time to put away what you've "decluttered."

Delegating tasks

The best way to get the job done when you're short on time is to let somebody else do it — delegate. In an office with staff at your disposal, this is relatively easy. You may simply give a copy of this book to your assistant, along with a priority list (desk first, and then files, and then calendar, and so on) and a timeline for what needs to be done by when. Or you could do the reading yourself, and then have a meeting with your office manager or staff to assign projects and establish deadlines.

At home, delegating can be a little bit harder. If you live alone, delegating is called *outsourcing*. If you have a spouse and/or children, delegating is referred to as *delicate family management*. Starting out as a team often helps, working side by side to purge and organize the toy collection and home media center or clean out the garage. Eventually, as your children (and your partner) grow up, you can hand off tasks altogether, which helps them grow up further.

Being accountable

Have you ever had someone assign you an important project upon which other people's decisions, schedules, or success rode? If so, you know what being accountable is like. The repercussions of a sloppy job or missed deadline could range from wrath or a ruptured relationship to losing a job. The result is that you work hard and fast. You can put the power of accountability to work in your organizing projects simply by telling someone — a sibling, spouse, colleague, neighbor, or friend — what you've promised yourself to do. Once you've told someone else your plan, you won't want to disappoint that person or look like a failure. Being accountable spurs achievement.

Want to make your accountability really stick? There are two ways to up the ante. One is to tell someone who truly cares about the outcome. Promise your boss you're going to clean off your desk, and I bet you won't delay. Say to your best friend or significant other, "I won't be late to meet you again because I'm finding ways to organize my time," and you may be doubly vested in planning your day. The second way is to set a definite date and/or time for your accountability buddy to call you back and ask you if you did what you said you would. Do you know how great it feels to say, "Yes"?

Pretending to move (or really moving)

Last but not least, a powerful motivator for getting organized is to move. When you consider the cost of moving all that extra junk, and the excess stress that your lack of planning and time-management systems will cause in the process, you'll get on the stick. No immediate plans to move? Well, you could make some in the interest of the cause — or just pretend. Set a real date for the move. Schedule it on your calendar, planning backward from the move date to today about what needs to be organized by when. Put the subgoals on your calendar too, and get moving!

Organizing your space

Organization takes place in space, and a question I commonly hear is, "Where do I start?" My answer is that you have two possibilities, depending upon the situation and your personal style. They are the following:

✔ **Beginning with the hot spot:** Choose your organizing space by selecting the place that frustrates or bothers you the most — the hot spot. After that, everything else will be downhill. If you go crazy every time you drive into the garage, spend your first organizing weekend creating a nice, welcoming home.

✔ **Starting slow and easy:** If the hot-spot approach has you splayed out on the couch in dread and defeat, simply turn 180 degrees and start in the space that's easiest for you.

Wherever you start, you want to work where the organization is taking place. Don't pull all your clothes out of the closet and take them into the living room to sort and toss; it requires an extra step and leaves you nowhere near a mirror or a rod for rehanging. You may need to clear off some space first because empty surfaces are vital to most organizing tasks. Make like a snowplow and push it all aside.

Organizing for the people who work, live, or play here

Organization is a people-based process, designed to make people happy and productive on a daily basis — so do ask "Who?" in all the organizing you do.

To personalize your organizing systems, ask yourself, "Who works, lives, or plays here?" What do they want and need? If you're reorganizing your file system, your new setup can affect whoever retrieves or files records there, so you might want to work with your assistant, staff, colleagues, or other family members to design the system together. At the very least, let them know what you've done. If you've just reorganized the pantry, a few labels are worth a thousand words in terms of guiding cohabitants to finding the snack center and putting the potato chips back. Are you single or in business for yourself? Use the tips in this book to organize in ways that work best for you but remember that you may also want to set up systems that meet client needs or make a visitor comfortable.

Getting organized is one of the most personal projects you can undertake in your life. Everyone thinks, acts, and feels differently, and no single system works for every person on the planet. If there was, someone would have packaged it into a pill long ago and I wouldn't have had the pleasure of writing this book.

How You Do It

This is a trick title because, of course, the rest of this book is about how to organize all the specifics of your life. But I'm training your mind here, so take this opportunity to discover how getting organized can be as simple as 1-2-3.

1. **Pick your target:** The good news is that getting organized can improve every aspect of your life. That's the bad news too, because you can't possibly do everything at once. The first step toward using my system to organize your life is choosing the target you want to start with. You've already established your mission and set your goals, so this presents no problem.

2. **Read this book:** Sit back, relax, and read. You can take notes or scribble in the margins. No matter what, you can find what you need to know and keep the text on hand as a reference all along the way.

3. **Schedule your organizing project:** Write your first organizing project in your calendar and set a deadline for completion. Match the length of the session to the scope of the task, whether the timeframe is 15 minutes or an hour a day, 3 hours a week, or a few work days or a weekend. Set aside the time on the schedule and go.

Maintaining Organization

Many people are hesitant to put the effort into getting organized because they doubt they can maintain an organized state of affairs. Like going on a diet, why bother if the excess pounds or clutter are just going to come back?

The beauty of getting organized is that it does retrain your mind, and there are no biochemical cues trying to confuse the message. In fact, organization is one of those self-reinforcing pleasures in which a mind and body, grateful for the reduced stress and strain, are eager to explore more. Enter maintenance.

If you follow the systems I describe, you may need to have a major organizing session only once a year or less to clean up any given area. A few basic tactics common to all these systems make maintenance easy. Here they are, for the benefit of your newly organizing mind:

- ✔ **Right now.** Clean up clutter as soon as you create it.
- ✔ **Every day.** Spend 15 minutes at the end of each day putting things away so tomorrow is a brand new start.

✔ **The one-year rule.** Every time you come across an object or piece of paper, ask yourself if you've used it in the past year. If the answer is no, chances are the item can go.

✔ **Plan and schedule.** If a major organizing job arises, don't sit around waiting to have the time to take on a grand action. Break it down into chunks today and write each upcoming task into your calendar.

✔ **Set routines.** Establish patterns, from the annual purging of everyone's closets before buying new school clothes and repaving the blacktop driveway to weekly grocery shopping, laundry, or housecleaning on the same day each week, and so on. Clean out the china cabinet and the garage each spring and fall. Write the car's oil changes into your calendar. Straighten up the house the day before its weekly cleaning. Purge a few files every day. The more routines that you can set, the faster and smoother things can go and the stronger your organizational systems can be.

✔ **Share.** Remember that maintenance isn't your job alone. Set up systems to share with or delegate to staff, family, and roommates.

The seeds are planted in your mind. All you need to do is fertilize them with all the information herein, and then watch your organized self blossom forth.

Chapter 2

Assembling the Tools, Supplies, and Systems

● ●

In This Chapter

▶ Systematizing space, work, information, and time

▶ Disposing in environmentally conscious ways

▶ Using containers to put everything in place

▶ Choosing right supplies and avoiding wrong ones

● ●

*G*etting organized is a systematic process, so it makes sense that there are some systems and supplies that go into making it work. On this subject, I have good news and good news. First, the right resources, from pullout drawers for your desktop to a calendar/planner matched to your scheduling needs, can make organizing far easier than you may have thought. Second, when you assemble the right resources to get organized, you don't need many. Some key containers and time-management tools, a small selection of information-management supplies, and six simple organizing procedures you can easily carry in your head to handle any organizing question are the sum total of what you need to change your life for the better.

Organizers and Planners: Lists to Live By

Organized people don't trust their memory — they trust their lists. Two lists can manage your time, plain and simple. You start with a *Master List,* which, just as it sounds, covers everything in your life, sort of an ongoing download from your mind. The Master List flows to your *To Do List,* the tool for scheduling your day, meeting your deadlines, and achieving your goals.

Once you have your lists in place, filling in your planner and putting it to work is as easy as pie. When you go shopping for your organizer, here are a few formats and names you may see.

- ✔ **Paper and paper-to-electronic systems:** At a Glance, DayTimers, Day Runners, Filofax, Franklin Covey. Old-fashioned paper has several advantages even in the twenty-first century: easy access, portability, and the ability to flip quickly and scan your schedule at a glance.

- ✔ **Electronic systems:** Palm Pilot and other portables (Casio, Hewlett Packard Jornada, and Royal daVinci) and various computer programs such as Microsoft Outlook. With the power to carry and categorize vast amounts of information, many electronic organizers also offer access to the Internet and e-mail via your Internet connection for computer programs, and through a wireless connection for portable devices.

You can spend anything from less than $10 to several hundred clams on an organizer, depending upon whether you choose paper or electronic and how many features and add-ons you want.

Though most organizing vendors are online, I recommend examining an actual organizer up close before you buy, to view what's on a page and determine which brand you want to try. If at first you don't succeed, try again with another type. Finding the one that works for you is worth the search, and fortunately, many organizer refills fit in other binders. Be sure to buy a size that you can carry around with you, because you may quickly discover that this single volume can contain your entire life.

Putting Things in Their Place: Containers

Every time you set out to organize a space, you need containers to clean out the deadwood and create homes for the survivors. Whether you're working in the garage or getting your office into shape, the following tools and techniques can help put everything into place.

No-strain containers: Types, shapes, and sizes

Containers can organize things by like type, such as trays for cosmetics or pens and pencils or dividers for desk or underwear drawers. They can keep food fresh, as a sealed canister does your pasta or pet food. Containers can facilitate cleanup — for instance, preschoolers' toys in big open baskets children can easily access. From the kitchen to the office, the board-room to the bath, containers are your organizing friends.

 Remember, don't dash out and go shopping yet. Just review some container basics here, and then later match the container to the job. I don't want you to end up with a closet full of unused crates because you really needed drawers instead.

Whenever you aim to contain, measure the item(s) and storage space first, and then search the house or hit the store for what you need. Containing options include:

- ✔ Cabinets
- ✔ Shelves
- ✔ Drawers and drawer dividers
- ✔ Bookcases and bookends
- ✔ Magazine racks
- ✔ File drawers and boxes
- ✔ Baskets, boxes, and a variety of closed containers
- ✔ Tiered and stacking racks

Each class of container comes in a range of materials, shapes, and sizes. Matching these characteristics to your containing criteria is your goal — so isn't it great that manufacturers have come out with just about every container you could ever need?

Selecting the material

In selecting material, consider the container's weight, durability, safety, and looks, and whether you can lift or carry it easily. In general, plastic is lightest, lasts long, and doesn't break. However, plastic is often not as scenic as glass or a pretty basket. You probably don't want plastic in your living room, but boy, is it great in the kitchen, inside cupboards, and for storage areas.

Choosing clear or colored containers

Clear containers have a clear advantage: You can see right through them to identify the contents inside. Unless you're trying to hide what's in your container, choose clear and save yourself a step. Transparent containers are also great for showing young children how to get organized. Seeing what's hiding inside — crayons, blocks, toy trucks — sends an easy visual cue for what gets put away there.

When visual neatness is your goal, go opaque with your containers to keep their contents hidden. In this case, you may want to use color as a code — for instance, a blue container to hold kids' gloves and green for adults'.

Doing geometry: Shape and size

Round containers waste space. Want to picture why? Square off a round container in your mind's eye, and you can see the corners that you're losing. Or put several round containers together and look at all the empty space in between. Whenever you can, choose squares or rectangles for your containers to avoid this geometric rip-off. Yes, you'll need some round bowls, and a big round basket works well for balls, but otherwise stick to the squares.

Once you have the basic geometry down, match the shape and size of containers to what you're storing there. Allow enough space to group things by like type, but not so much that things get lost or jumbled within the container or you're left with a lot of room to spare.

Also ask yourself whether you need a lid on this container. Does it need a tight seal or stackable surface? Some containers, such as Tupperware's Modular Mates, stack easily on top of each other, which can make good use of vertical space.

If you're containing food, you might consider a pouring spout. Try this concept on your containers for cereal, sugar, rice, pancake mix, and biscuit mix.

Identifying with labels

A label can save loads of time by identifying a container's contents with a quick look. Best for things you're storing out of sight (nobody wants to sit on the living room couch and read a label that says "Extra Ashtrays"), container labels add information to your organization. Here are a few tips:

✔ Be sure to use a washable label if you may be cleaning the container in question (for instance, the one you store your flour in). Skip the white computer labels and use a clear, plastic one or a tape made on a label-maker instead.

✔ Clear labels are hard to see on clear containers. If you use a clear, washable label on a clear container per the preceding point, place the label low so that the contents behind it can serve as a background.

> ✔ Use colored labels to code containers by type.
> Maybe all your baking supplies are in containers
> with blue labels ("b" is for blue and for baking),
> while pasta and grains are labeled with green
> ("g" for green and grains).

Just as firefighters talk about containing fires, use containers to contain clutter and spend less time putting out organizational fires. Containers provide a place for every important item in your life.

The Three Ds: Using containers as clutter busters

A major contributor to clutter is a basic law of physics: Matter is inert. The way to unclutter is to make matter mobile, and the Three Ds can help. What are the Three Ds? Three containers — boxes, baskets, or big sturdy bags — that you use anytime you tackle a space to distribute, donate, or dump the stuff you find there. Here's how the Three Ds can ease the flow of things and keep you clutter-free.

Distribute box

Have you ever noticed how things tend to end up where they don't belong? To bring them on home, take a container and dub it "Distribute." When you find a cereal bowl in the bedroom, don't rush downstairs to take it to the kitchen, and then go back up to collect the dirty clothes and run them down to the laundry room, followed by a stop in the front hall to grab the suntan lotion you had out for yesterday's tennis game and return it to the upstairs linen closet, and so on and so on until you're utterly exhausted. Five minutes of simple cleanup can wipe you out for the day unless you centralize operations with a distribute box.

Any time you need to leave the room to put something away, don't. Put it in the distribute box instead, and then carry it along to the next stop, just like riders on the bus waiting to exit until they reach home.

Donate box

Maybe the item is not out of place but it no longer has a place in your life. When that's the case, consider donating. Anything useable but no longer useful to you goes in the donate box, which sits there waiting to go to your sister, neighbor, or your favorite charity for a tax write-off. For instance, if you have three sizes of clothes in your closet, you obviously aren't wearing two of them, so donate those. You probably don't want to go back to the larger size, and when you reach the smaller one, you'll deserve a treat of some new clothes in today's styles. The same goes for appliances, equipment (donate or sell computer stuff the second it gets disconnected from your system; those things aren't getting any younger), dishes, furniture — you name it. Letting things move on to people who can use them makes the world a better place, and your donate box can help.

Dump box, bag, or can

Then there are things that nobody wants or needs. You can designate a box, trash can, or big garbage bag for things you choose to dump as you unclutter. The trick is to keep it close at hand as you work and put anything

you want to discard directly into the garbage.
Don't forget to recycle when you can. Garage
sales, consignment stores, and charities are
great ways to recycle.

You can organize your giveaways by establishing a
donation center in the basement or another storage
area where you collect things until you have enough
to warrant a pickup or a trip to a drop-off center.

The Six Organizing Secrets

Every professional organizer has her or his secrets, and
when I was invited to write this book, the publisher
asked me to give away mine. So here they are: six sure-
fire ways to think through organizing any space or job,
from the dining room to the desktop, from tomorrow's
meeting to where you want your marriage to be five
years from now.

Five of the organizing secrets are *acronyms,* words in
which each letter stands for a step of the process to
make each one easy to remember. Technically, this is
called a *mnemonic device,* also known as a way to help
your memory. Whether you remember the technical
term or not, this is a very organized way to think, and
simply remembering the six organizing secrets and
putting the secrets to work can help train your organizing mind.

Designing any space with a layout

When you start out to tackle a space, the ideal first
question takes in the big picture: "Where do things go?"
Is that the best arrangement for the desk and filing

cabinets? Can you open up more space by moving the bed? What's the most efficient use of the room's wall space? To answer the big picture question, I simply ask you to think like an architect.

Even if you've never sat down at a drafting table, you can lay out any space by drawing, cutting, and playing. So make like an architect and create your own blueprint for high-performance rooms. Just follow these simple steps:

1. **Draw the basic blueprint:** First, get out a tape measure and measure the dimensions of the space you want to organize, including the width of each wall, window, door, and closet, as well as the height underneath windows. Jot down each measurement as you go.

   Now swap your tape measure for a ruler and draw your room to scale on a blank piece of paper, using 1 inch to represent 1 foot. Tape two sheets of paper together if you need to. After sketching the basic outline, mark the windows, including a note about the wall clearance underneath, the closets, and the doors.

2. **Create cutouts:** Now think about what furniture and equipment you want in the room, which may include what's there now or something that's been on your wish list. Measure these items if you already have them or estimate their dimension if not. Next, take some colored paper and cut out a rectangle, square, or circle to represent each

piece, again using 1 inch to represent 1 foot as your scale. A typical desk is about 6 feet long and 3 feet wide, so that becomes a 6-x3-inch rectangular cutout.

3. **Play with your layout:** Finally, put glue that allows you to reposition your layout on the backs of the cutouts so you can move them around on your blueprint but not lose their place, and play with your layout. Remember to use the space under windows for smaller pieces — a desk or two-drawer file cabinet in an office, or a dresser or short bookcase in the home. Also keep in mind that doors need room to open and close, so don't put the fax machine in the door's path.

Keep playing until you come up with one or more layouts you like. You may discover a whole new look for your room, or that there's not enough space for the bedroom and bureau to share a wall, all without lifting a finger or straining your back. Not bad for your first organizing secret.

Saving or tossing

From clothes bursting out of closets to the constant assault of information, most people in our affluent part of the world are buried in a daily inflow and existing excess of stuff. How do you decide what to keep and what's a waste of space and time — not to mention energy and money? Simply ask the five W-A-S-T-E questions, and you're well on your way to an informed keep-or-toss decision.

I know from my experience as a professional organizer that the process of deciding what matters in your life and what to let go of goes as deep as it gets. I developed W-A-S-T-E to help separate the wheat from the chaff. As you work through the questions, think like a judge, considering past precedent, future ramifications, and sometimes subjective differences between right and wrong:

- ✔ **Worthwhile:** Do you truly like the dress or shirt in question? Is that article actually important to your job? Does the fax cover sheet contain any information you need to know? If the item isn't worthwhile, toss it out now. If it is, move on to the next four questions.

- ✔ **Again:** Will you really use this thing again, or is it just going to sit in a kitchen cupboard or take up space in your files? This question could also be rephrased as, "Use it or lose it." If you don't foresee needing something in the next year or you haven't used it in the last one, clear it out. Maybe your waffle iron was used weekly for awhile but hasn't been touched in months because you broke up with the boyfriend you cooked them for or got tired of cleaning out the grooves. It was once worthwhile, but now, goodbye!

- ✔ **Somewhere else:** Ask yourself: Can I easily find this somewhere else? If you have to make waffles for a special brunch, can you borrow a maker from a neighbor? Can you find a memo in your assistant's files or in another department, or get the details by making a quick phone call? Can you hit the Internet, the library, or the local discount store if the need for this item or info should arise in the future? If so, you don't need to save it. Sometimes, the somewhere else is quite close at hand, such as in your own closet, cupboard, or office. Do you really need half a dozen fix-it outfits for painting or messy plumbing jobs when you only wear one at a time?

✔ **Toss:** Many things have ways of slipping and sliding by the first three questions, so here's the acid test: Will anything happen if you toss it? If not, go ahead, unless it must be legally retained.

✔ **Entire:** Do you need the entire thing? The whole magazine, document, or draft? Every coordinate of the outfit, even if you only ever wear the pants? The complete catalog, when you only intend to order from one page? If not, keep what you need and toss the excess.

Everything is the sum of its parts, but some parts count more than others. Use the entire question to trim the things you do keep down to size.

Everything in its P-L-A-C-E: Organizing space

In the course of my practice, I've developed a reliable process to clear an area of clutter, organize items for easy access and neat appearance, and fine-tune the results to your needs. P-L-A-C-E is the way to organize space and put everything in its place. What could be easier to remember?

You can clean up any area in the world with the follow-ing five steps:

- ✔ **Purge:** First, break out the Three Ds and the five W-A-S-T-E questions and clear your space of clutter by dumping, donating, or distributing everything you no longer need. Whether you toss the dried-up glue sticks in your desk drawer, discard outgrown toys in the playroom, or clean the hall closet of unmatched gloves and ratty old sweatshirts, purging can empower all your organ-izing efforts.

- ✔ **Like with like:** The second step in putting things into place is to organize like things together. Not only does grouping help you know where to look, whether you're searching for a file or a first aid lotion but placing similar items together also often creates what I call centers, one-stop spots with everything you need to complete a task.

- ✔ **Access:** Once you have things grouped, placement is the next priority — and here, think easy access. Where do you usually use these items? Put them there. Pots and pans should be near the stove and file cabinets close to your desk. How close is close? Literally at your fingertips.

- ✔ **Contain:** Containers do double duty from an organizing perspective: They keep like things together, and move things out of sight to clear the landscape and your mind. You can contain things on shelves, in drawers, with bookends or maga-zine holders, in hanging files, or in baskets, boxes, or closed containers in a variety of materials, shapes, and sizes. Contain within containers by adding dividers to drawers. The more you contain, the better you may feel.

✔ **Evaluate:** After you complete the first four steps of P-L-A-C-E, Evaluate: Does it work? Organization is an ongoing process, and organizing can often be improved upon as your needs change or you sharpen your skills.

When you evaluate and adjust over time, your organization systems become self-maintaining. Some good occasions to assess your systems include job changes, starting college, getting your first apartment, getting married, getting divorced, and any time you move. But you don't have to wait for these major events to evaluate. A yearly checkup can help you keep everything working at peak level and up-to-date with your current needs.

Clearing your desktop with R-E-M-O-V-E

One very common reason people call me is that they can't see the surface of their desk and have no idea how to fix the situation short of a snowplow. That's why I developed R-E-M-O-V-E, six steps to clear off even the most snowed-under desktop and set a desk up for success:

✔ **Reduce distractions:** Is your desk covered with pictures, knickknacks, or this morning's mail? These may be distracting you and reducing productivity. The reduce principle helps you to identify distractions and get them off your desk.

- ✔ **Everyday use:** Only things that you use every day may stay on top of your desk. Don't worry; you'll find homes for everything else you need.

- ✔ **Move to the preferred side:** You use one hand for most daily operations, and your desk can be arranged accordingly. Placing pens, pencils, and pads where you reach for them most gives you fingertip management and makes everything from writing notes to taking phone calls faster and easier.

- ✔ **Organize together:** Just as with P-L-A-C-E, organizing like things together on the desktop forms centers so you can find and use items easily.

- ✔ **View your time:** Everybody hates to be late, so give yourself a leg up by making time visual on your desk. An organizer and a clock are important desktop elements for keeping time in view.

- ✔ **Empty the center:** Finally, chanting my mantra that "The desk is a place to do work," clear off a space in the center of the station so that you can work on the project at hand. Behold, a long-lost surface — your desk.

Responding to your mail with R-A-P-I-D

Even before e-mail came on the scene, mail overload had slowed many people down to snail's pace, so this system is designed to help you pick up speed with a R-A-P-I-D sort that doesn't even require opening an envelope. Five sort categories help you bring order to incoming mail and get it opened and filed in a flash. Here they are:

✔ **Read:** Anything that you need to read — later, please — goes in this stack. You may often find to read items at the bottom of the mail pile because they're big ol' magazines and newsletters.

✔ **Attend:** Notices and invitations for seminars, workshops, meetings, performances, parties, and so forth go in the to attend stack.

✔ **Pay:** If somebody wants your money, to pay is the pile to put the item in. Window envelopes are an easy cue. If it looks like one more credit card offer you don't want, just rip right through the envelope to protect your identity and toss, all without taking the time to open it. Time is money, and all these folks are already after yours.

✔ **Important:** Presume important until proven innocent, and put all unknown incoming mail into this stack.

✔ **Dump:** If you know at a glance that you won't read or need it, do not break the seal on the envelope. Do dump that piece of mail in the nearest available trash can.

Maximizing your time with P-L-A-N

The most important thing you can plan is your time, that precious and irreplaceable commodity. Yes, there's more to it than simply marking dates in your calendar but planning time doesn't have to be hard. All you need are four steps formulated to take you to your goals, large or small, soon or later on. Put time on your side and achieve your peak potential with the power of P-L-A-N.

- ✔ **Prepare:** The step you all too often skip in dividing up your time on Earth is defining missions and setting goals. The result can be that instead of pursuing what you want and need, you simply do whatever presents itself to you. Prepare repairs this problem by taking you through the "Five W's Plus How," forming the foundation for plans from next week's party to long-range career development or finding the love of your life.

- ✔ **Lists you can live by:** Out of your goals flow things to do, and the Master and To Do Lists keep track of all these tasks over the short and long term so you can do more and stress less. Once you find out how to use these lists along with your daily planner, you need never let a small detail or top priority slip again.

- ✔ **Act with rhythms and routines:** Time has rhythms, like the ticking of the clock, the beating of your heart, and the biochemical changes your body and brain go through every day. When you learn to act with your personal rhythms and establish time-saving routines, you may find more minutes in the day and reap better results from all your efforts. From sleeping to peaking to pacing, acting with rhythms and routines helps you go with the flow.

✔ **Notice and reward your accomplishments:** Here comes the fun part: Whenever you accomplish a goal, you earn yourself a reward, and the P-L-A-N system makes sure you get one by building a prize right into the time management process. When you notice and reward your accomplishments, you create an even stronger incentive to reach your goal the next time around. Pretty soon you have a positive feedback loop that can spiral you right to the moon.

By now, you know why you want to get organized. You have a plan for tackling organization in your mind. You've met the systems and supplies, so you can expect no confusing surprises as you work with this guidebook in the priority order of your choice. You know what you need to know. So what are you waiting for? Go!

Chapter 3

Scheduling Skills for Maximum Productivity

• •

In This Chapter

▶ Getting to know how to flow

▶ Delegating tasks, preventing interruptions

▶ Tasking techniques

▶ Making the most of the phone and other tricks

• •

"**D**o not squander time, that is the stuff life is made of," Benjamin Franklin said. So imagine you're in traffic, trying to get from here to there. What one thing squanders the most time of your trip? The red light.

Red lights are all around you in life, making you stop and wait as the minutes tick by, adding time to every task that could have been saved if only you were driving in synch with optimal traffic flow.

Time management is the way to green-light your day, eliminating obstacles and time wasters to give you the go signal every step of the way. You may have already made a plan. But because even the best laid plans can go awry, you need green-light techniques to put your plans into action without the sudden stops that can come between you and your goals. Think green . . . and become a time-maximizing machine.

Going with the Flow: The Time Log

Flow is in, and for good reason. Whether you're driving a car or playing basketball, churning out a report or researching torts, the ability to get in the groove so that you're working with time instead of against it is key to peak productivity. Psychologists call this transcendent marriage between time and the mind *flow,* and when you get flow, you're good to go.

To find flow, you have to take control of your time and eliminate the interruptions and time wasters so common to the average day.

The first step is to find out how you actually spend your time by keeping a Time Log. A record of all the time you spend on every little thing, from the moment you rise in the morning until you put your head down on the pillow at night, the Time Log is a powerful tool for discovering how you allocate the minutes and hours of your life. Be prepared for good news and bad. I'll give you the bad news first: Unless you're practicing good time management or are a very exceptional person, you probably waste a fair amount of time. The good news is that once you find that time, you can reclaim it. The extra minutes and hours are a free gift from me to you, no strings attached.

To start your Time Log, take a sheet of ruled paper. In the left-hand margin, note the time you change activities, and on the line to the right list exactly what you're doing: getting ready for work or bed, commuting, doing projects or paperwork, making calls, talking to visitors, attending meetings, reading mail, making or eating meals, walking the dog, watching TV, and so on. Also note who else was involved so you can later determine how relevant each activity was to your goals and who tends to take up your time the most.

If you'd like to try a different method, you can create a spreadsheet on the computer, making each row on the sheet represent a 15-minute time block. Many people find this easier because the blocks remind them to log what they were doing. Accounting for time accurately on the computer spreadsheet can be harder, however, because not all activities neatly fall into 15-minute blocks.

Whether you go manual or electronic, keep your Time Log for at least several days in a row, and optimally for a whole week including a weekend to provide a complete picture of how different days go. I know logging your activities and the time taken is somewhat of a hassle, but hey — just pretend you're a high-paid lawyer. Attorneys always log their time.

Fixing Your Flow: The Busters

When your log is complete, take a good look to see where the time went. Total up your time by activity type, both for each day and for the whole week. Are you spending time on things according to your priorities? Does anything stand out? Too much time on the phone? Too little time for yourself or with your family or friends or on your current key project?

How much time did you spend procrastinating? How many interruptions did you have? What kind? Who were they with? Are there things you shouldn't have been doing because the activities could have been delegated or you simply should have said, "No"?

Can you bundle certain activities together? Are you going out to run errands twice in one day when they can be consolidated into one trip? Could you get all your paperwork out of the way at once? Can you set aside a morning to take care of client calls?

Take a red pen and circle anything that was, in light of your values and goals, a waste of time, even a meeting with your boss or a phone call to a friend. How can you get these time wasters out of your day?

Procrastination busters: Read this now

You can't get flow without getting started, and starting is often the hardest part. For most people, procrastination isn't a result of laziness or lack of resolve. Procrastination can be a deep psychological situation involving fear of failure or success, or a natural result of overload. Sometimes you simply don't know where to start.

Procrastination is such a widespread problem that I make a point of providing excellent ways to beat it in my workshops and training. First, consider whether you tend to do better when working with other people or relying on yourself. Then choose your technique.

Involving other people

There are four ways (A, B, C, and D) that you can call on other people to help you do what you ought to be doing. Choose one or as many as it takes.

- ✔ **Be accountable:** Tell someone what you're going to do and by when. Accountability is built into many tasks at work, in which you have to report to a boss or a team, but try telling your best friend too. At home, see how you hop to cleaning the garage after you tell your buddy Jerry the garage will be spic and span by Sunday night. Better yet, invite Jerry to stop by around 5 p.m. on Sunday to inspect your handiwork. Fill your office mate in on your plan to finish project XYZ, and by all means, tell your mother about your vow to start saving $200 a month.

- ✔ **Barter:** If you procrastinate because you don't like or know your task very well, simply swap jobs with someone. Maybe you can type like the wind, but don't really get or care how spreadsheet formulas work. Tell your colleague Joyce, the local spreadsheet whiz, that you'll type up a report for her if she'll handle your spreadsheet formulas. It's a win-win!

- ✔ **Collaborate:** Working with someone else can help get the job started and done faster because you now have a shared commitment and two minds or pairs of hands. You may assemble a team to divvy up different parts of a project, or ask a friend to come over for your annual closet cleanout to help you decide what looks good and what can go to charity or the resale shop.

✔ **Delegate:** Why do the task yourself when someone else can? Supervisors should delegate tasks to staff so that employees can grow in their jobs. Parents can teach children household jobs and self-management skills that help them discover the meaning of responsibility and feel like contributing members of the family.

Doing it yourself

If you need or prefer to lean on yourself to beat the procrastination trap, there are plenty of solo ways to jump-start your motor. Look for a match with your personality style in the techniques that follow:

✔ **Jump in!:** Have you ever noticed how kids get in the pool? Youngsters generally run to the deep end and just jump in without checking the temperature because there's nothing kids can do to change it and they want to go swimming. The faster you get in, the faster you get used to the water, so just jump.

✔ **Take it step by step:** Of course, under no circumstances will you ever see me jump into the pool. You can find me down at the other end, slowly walking down the steps and taking my time getting used to the water temperature as each part of my body, from my feet to my stomach to my chest, gets wet. Any project can be achieved the same way, one step at a time so take a small step today.

✔ **Choose your starting point:** You don't always have to start at the so-called beginning or proceed in linear order. If you want to start a project on page three, start on page three. If you plan a holiday dinner and you'd rather design the menu before you decide on the guest list, that's fine. Just go back and figure quantities after you know how many you're having.

✔ **Race the clock:** When we were kids, my brother and I used to race to see who could drink their milk the fastest. Chances are you raced the clock in college by pulling an all-nighter to write a paper or study for finals. Deadlines drive achievement, so give yourself one, write down the date and time you want to finish, and race the clock.

✔ **Tie yourself down:** As a last resort, you need to simply tie yourself down. Tell yourself you can't go to the movies, you can't watch TV, you can't even get a cup of coffee until you write that report or paint that room. Pretend there's a real rope holding you there, and you literally can't leave until you do what you have to do. You can even use a tie or scarf to strap yourself to the chair. You may think twice before taking that coffee break.

Interruption busters: Phone calls and visitors

So you finally get going on your project and what happens? Interruptions. Flow's greatest enemy and a pervasive part of modern living, interruptions eat time twice over, both the minutes or hours interruptions take and the time required to regain your focus when they're over. Even if you can stop an interruption in progress, you still need to refocus, so prevent uninvited disturbances before they begin.

✔ **Telephone:** The simplest way to stop telephone interruptions is not to pick up the receiver when the phone rings or when you think you'll just clear up a point with a quick call and end up talking for half an hour.

✔ **Visitors:** Visitors may not be as common an interruption as the telephone, but a real live person can be more compelling. You can discover ways to control visitor traffic in the next section.

Strategies for work

Diplomacy is key when carving out quiet time at work. Just remember that at the end of the day, your staff, colleagues, and superiors will respect you more for getting your job done than for being always available.

✔ **Screen.** Have an assistant or receptionist greet your visitors and tell the unexpected or noncritical ones that you're in a meeting.

✔ **Close.** Sometimes cutting yourself off is hard, but a closed door is a clear signal to all those who pass that you're busy on the other side. For those who still knock, open the door partway only and ask them to come back at a specific time. Don't let the visitor start the conversation.

- ✔ **Stand.** If you don't have a door or closing the door is not appropriate, greet incoming visitors by standing up. Most people won't sit down if you stand.

- ✔ **Walk.** So you're on your feet but your guest is reclining in your favorite chair. Now's the time to suggest that you chat while walking back to your visitor's desk, or say that you have somewhere to go. Then do go, preferably to the restroom, where only the most intrepid will tag along.

- ✔ **Hide.** Who says you have to work where people can find you? Go to a conference room, an empty office, a corporate or offsite library, or your home office for high-intensity times. Only the true bloodhounds will track you down.

- ✔ **Sign.** Put up a sign on your door or cubicle wall that says, "Do Not Disturb — Important Project." Depending upon your relationship with others in the office, people may respectfully leave you alone or take every opportunity to taunt you.

- ✔ **Postpone.** For hard cases, schedule an appointment to talk about an issue later, or a lunch to catch up on the social front.

Schedule appointments you'd rather not take before meetings so you have a good excuse to leave. If your time log reveals a particular person who repeatedly interrupts you throughout the day, schedule a daily 15- to 30-minute meeting to answer all the questions at once.

Strategies for home-based businesses

When you work at home, visitor interruptions all too often come from people you love. That doesn't mean you have to let flow go down the drain.

- ✔ **Business hours.** Inform family members of your work schedule (9 to 5 for most) and ask that they only disturb you for very important matters or emergencies.

- ✔ **Signs that speak volumes.** Put a sign on the door during important or peak times that says "Quiet, Do Not Disturb." If the sign is printed on colored paper, even children who can't read will know what the words mean. Red, hot pink, neon green — just be sure to share your color code with your cohabitants.

- ✔ **Outsource meetings.** Hosting a meeting at home can be less than professional and cause you to spend hours cleaning up. Instead, arrange to meet clients or customers at their office. If this isn't possible, rent a conference room or choose a mutually convenient coffeehouse.

- ✔ **No-pet policy.** Much as you may love them, corral pets away from your office so barking dogs or mewing cats don't interrupt your concentration or telephone calls.

- ✔ **Nobody's home.** Don't answer the door during working hours unless you're waiting for a special delivery. Use a peephole if you need to know.

Strategies for home

Just because you're home doesn't mean you're available. Remember the value of your time when visitors knock, and don't spend your time on just anyone.

- ✔ **Who's there?** Peer out your peephole to check the identity of unexpected visitors, and don't answer to those you don't know.

- ✔ **Not interested.** Don't waste time talking to salespeople when you have no intention of buying something from them. Once you know what they want, politely say "No" and let them go ring someone else's door or phone.

- ✔ **Stay focused.** If you're doing something that can't be interrupted, such as baking a cake or surfing the Net, just let the doorbell ring. No one has to know you're home unless you're expecting something important. How often does necessary news arrive at your door?

Occupational overload: Just say "No"

Once you beat procrastination and interruptions, you have to get to the meat of the time-management matter: One of the biggest reasons work doesn't get done is that there is simply too much of it. Sometimes the biggest favor you can do for everyone involved is to say "No." Here are four steps that help:

1. **Listen and understand the request.** What's being asked of you and why? You have to really understand the request to say a "No" that will stick.

2. **Say "No."** I know saying "No" is easier said than done, but just start with an "n" sound, and then put your mouth in the shape of an "o" and say "No, I'm sorry, I can't do it."

3. **Give reasons.** Simply and clearly state the reasons that you can't do the project or go to the meeting or be on the organization's board. "No, I'm sorry, I can't do it because I have three other commitments."

4. **Suggest alternatives.** If you understand the what and why behind the request, suggesting another way or someone else who may be able to do it is easier. "No, I'm sorry. I can't, but Jean knows about that matter and she can help you."

Saying "No" to your boss, of course, is always a bit of a special case. You can suggest someone else to do the project, but if the boss still wants you to do it, then you need to explain the work that you currently have.

"I would need to stop working on Project A to do Project B. Do you want me to do that?" or "I already have Projects A, B, and C to do. What are the priorities?" Your boss may be glad for the assist with prioritizing, and you may be glad to have a workload that allows you to perform at your best.

Delegating: The four Ds

Of course, there's an alternative to saying "No" that's often the right thing to do: Delegate. Passing a task along to someone else in a more appropriate position to do it can maximize the value of everybody's time.

Whether an expert who knows something you don't, somebody under you whose time costs less, or a colleague with time to spare when you're in a crunch, delegating to the right person can be more efficient all around than taking on every task that crosses your path. To delegate is not to dump — delegating is to assign a task in a clear, productive way. To do so, follow the four Ds of Delegation as follows:

✔ **Decide what to delegate and to whom:** The right time to pass a job along is when you face any of the following types of tasks: routine, technical, short, those you don't have time for, and those that train others.

  An expert can often do specialized jobs better, from writing a computer routine to serving dinner for 50. Experts may cost more, but if they can do it faster and better than you can, you may save money and time at the bottom line. Calculate what your time is worth and compare it to the cost of hiring out.

✔ **Direct what, not how:** Tell the delegate what you want done — the end objective of the job. But unless you're teaching a brand-new skill, don't dictate how to do the job itself. People learn more and are better motivated when they can figure things out for themselves. Communication is very important when you're delegating, so go to a quiet place such as a meeting room or your office with the door closed so the delegate can listen intently to explanations and ask questions afterward. Get feedback to confirm that your goal is clear.

✔ **Define authority:** Tell your delegate exactly how much authority you're granting. Is there a dollar limit on the project? A decision point at which you must be consulted? Defining authority helps the delegate do the best job within the bounds you consider appropriate.

✔ **Deadlines:** I discussed how deadlines help get work completed. Now turn the tables. Let the delegates tell you when they can a) give you a progress report and b) deliver a final product. If you have a deadline on your end, make sure their due date is earlier in case they need extra time or you need to correct something.

It's How You Do It: Strategic Tasking

Say you put procrastination behind you. Eliminated interruptions. Used delegation and the word no to trim your task list to a manageable load. It's time to get down to work, so what's the best way? Strategic tasking is the art and science of matching the type of job to your manner of approach.

Single tasking

To *single-task* is to truly work on one thing at a time. When you want to focus and concentrate on something big, hard, or new, single tasking is the mode to use.

Group tasking

Grouping many tasks that are small and/or routine according to the principle of *like* can allow you to expedite routine work most efficiently. The more you repeat an activity, the easier and faster it gets.

Group tasking gets things done faster through the power of repetition. Here are the jobs to group together to make the most of your time: paying bills, opening incoming mail, reading incoming e-mail, tackling correspondence, writing thank-you notes, updating data entry and your contact entry files (name, address, phone), and running errands.

Multitasking: Personal calls and waiting

Then there are the moments in which you can and should be doing more than one thing at once. I'd like to chime in that I sincerely believe that you can only do one thing at a time well, but how well do you need to wait in line? Multitasking has become a way of modern life because people have more to do, including low-grade but necessary jobs that don't deserve full attention. Here's where to double up.

Personal calls plus

Given that no one can seem to spend a nanosecond off the phone anymore, why not take advantage of wireless technology to do two things at once? Enjoy guilt-free social calls by tucking a cordless phone under your chin or donning a headset and completing routine tasks such as cooking a meal, cleaning, straightening up, doing your nails, or watering the plants. This dual task paradigm does not extend to more demanding activities such as interfacing with your children or walking on the treadmill. Nobody needs to hear you panting or playing a game while they're spending their precious time trying to talk to you. And don't double up on business calls. It's a quick way to lose respect and miss important information.

Waiting and in transit

At appointments, in line at the post office, at a lunch engagement, in the subway station — you probably spend hours waiting every month of your life. Get that time back by tasking while you wait.

- ✔ **Read.** Don't go anywhere you'll need to wait without a part of your *To Read File* or your current book in hand. Not only is this a productive and/or pleasant way to pass the time, but you may find that reading in different environs sparks new ideas. Take a plastic file folder with just as much reading as you think you may have time for.

- ✔ **Write.** Quick notes such as thank yous, birthday, or catch-up cards are a great way to tick items off your list while you wait. Keep a few assorted note cards in a plastic folder and take the folder along for the extra time you find at the doctor's office or before a workshop.

- ✔ **E-mail.** If you have a laptop or handheld computer, reading and responding to e-mail is a good waiting game, because you can usually find an easy stopping point.

> ✔ **Plan.** There's nothing like waiting to help you remember all the things you need to do so take this time to work on your Master or To Do List.

Any time you leave the office or home, ask yourself what you can do on the way. Could you drop off the dry cleaning on the way to work, pick up some office supplies en route to a meeting, take advantage of an out-of-the-way appointment to get to your favorite antique store?

Pro Communications

All the time management in the world won't help you get things done if you can't communicate effectively. Whether getting the message across is your job — you could be in sales, a teacher, or a mom — or you work on a committee or team, get or receive assignments, assist someone, administer a program, or are simply trying to get along with your roommates, mastering the art of interpersonal contacts will save you time and make your day much nicer.

The phone: Incoming calls and messages

The first question to ask yourself about incoming calls is, "Am I taking them?" A quick reminder from the previous section on interruptions: You don't have to answer the phone just because it rings. Voice mail, caller ID, answering machines, and assistants are all available to put you in control of your incoming calls — which, from a time-management perspective, is the only place to be.

The busiest days for incoming telephone calls are Mondays. If you can screen calls, Monday is definitely the day to do it.

For people in sales, public relations, consulting, and speaking, voice-mail screening may not be a viable option. Prospective clients shopping for services or media people looking for a news lead may choose whomever they reach first on the phone, so you could miss the boat by calling back

 When you talk to new callers, be sure to get their direct-dial number so you can save going through a switchboard or assistant if you ever have to call them back.

The outgoing message on your voice-mail or answering machine is your calling card to everyone who calls you. Make a good impression and elicit important information from your callers with a *power message*. What's a power message? One you script, rehearse, and deliver with enthusiasm. Type up all the messages you use and keep the sheet in your Phone/Voice-mail File. Pull the file out anytime you need to record a new message, and you can have a power greeting in place in seconds.

Playing and taking messages

It absolutely amazes me how many people play their messages back and then save them. Talk about double work. The save button should be called spend instead, which is what it does with your time. Play the message once, write it down, and then erase it. If you miss a name or number, repeat the message right then and there.

Note the magic words *write it down* in the preceding paragraph. Writing is of course critical if you take messages for others, but even if you listen to a personal answering machine at home and you live alone, you need to write down every message you receive in order to green-light your day.

All messages you need to act upon can go on your Master List as soon as you get them. Skip straight to your To Do List if you plan to act today.

Handling outgoing calls effectively

Before you pick up the phone, stop and ask: Is there a better way? If you only need to disseminate information rather than discuss it, a fax or an e-mail may be faster. Human beings are chatty by nature. If discussion is required simply to set up a meeting time or find out a fact or two, delegate the call to an assistant, if you can. For those calls you do need to make, don't just grab the receiver at random. Have a calling plan.

Use the program and speed-dial features on all your phones, cellular and regular. That's fingertip management of your phone calls! You can also use the dial function on computer contact-management programs connected to your phone, then have that person's record open and ready to receive your notes.

Choosing your time

Prime time for outgoing calls is 9 to 11 in the morning and 2 to 4 in the afternoon. This allows for the average arrival, departure, and lunch hours for most work places, though some stores and doctor's offices don't open until after 10 a.m. and many consumer-oriented businesses are open into the evening.

Calling outside of prime time can be a great strategy if you are a) hoping to reach voice mail instead of the person, or b) trying to reach somebody who's been waylaying you with an assistant. Many executives answer their own phones before or after hours when their assistants aren't in. (Of course if they've read this book, they'll plan their time better. If you were high on their priority list they would have already called you back, and if not they shouldn't be talking to you anyway.)

Note the time zone you call and adjust accordingly. Most phone books have a time zone map in the front, as do many organizers.

Take advantage of off-peak phone rates and time zone differences by making long-distance calls East early in the morning and West in the evening.

Try setting a certain time each day to pick up your messages and return calls. You may want to have one peak and one off-peak time, depending upon whether calls are important or routine.

Organizing and prioritizing your calls

Consider what calls are the most important today and mark their priority order on your To Do List, accounting for any time zone differences. Gather all of the relevant material you need for all your calls, which usually includes your datebook/organizer, any relevant papers, and perhaps your To Discuss List. If you have several issues to cover, start with the most important items on the list so that if the other person is suddenly called away, your top priorities have been taken care of.

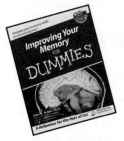

With more than 1,300 titles to choose from, we've got a Dummies Book for wherever you are in life!

Dummies Books — Plain-English Solutions for Everyday Challenges

Home & Business Computer Basics

Excel 2007 All-in-One Desk Reference For Dummies	9780470037386	$29.99/$35.99 CAN
MacBook For Dummies	9780470048597	$21.99/$25.99 CAN
Office 2007 All-in-One Desk Reference For Dummies	9780471782797	$29.99/$35.99 CAN
PCs All-in-One Desk Reference For Dummies, 4th Edition	9780470223383	$29.99/$35.99 CAN
PCs For Dummies, 11th Edition	9780470137284	$21.99/$25.99 CAN
Troubleshooting Your PC For Dummies	9780764516696	$24.99/$37.99 CAN
Upgrading & Fixing PCs For Dummies	9780764516658	$21.99/$32.99 CAN
Windows XP All-in-One Desk Reference For Dummies	9780471749417	$29.99/$35.99 CAN
Windows Vista For Dummies	9780471754213	$21.99/$25.99 CAN
Windows Vista For Dummies, Quick Reference	9780471783268	$16.99/$19.99 CAN
Word 2007 For Dummies	9780470036587	$21.99/$25.99 CAN
CD & DVD Recording For Dummies	9780764516276	$21.99/$32.99 CAN

Internet & Digital Media

Digital Photography All-in-One Desk Reference For Dummies, 3rd Edition	9780470037430	$35.99/$47.99 CAN
Geneology For Dummies	9780764508073	$24.99/$37.99 CAN
Internet All-in-One Desk Reference For Dummies	9780764516597	$29.99/$44.99 CAN
Internet For Dummies, 11th Edition	9780470121740	$21.99/$25.99 CAN
Search Engine Optimization For Dummies, 2nd Edition	9780471979982	$24.99/$29.99 CAN
iPhone For Dummies	9780470174692	$21.99/$25.99 CAN
AppleTV For Dummies	9780470173626	$21.99/$25.99 CAN
Photoshop Elements 2 For Dummies	9780764516757	$21.99/$32.99 CAN
YouTube For Dummies	9780470149256	$21.99/$25.99 CAN

Graphics & Web Development

Flash CS3 For Dummies	9780470121009	$24.99/$29.99 CAN
ASP.NET For Dummies	9780764508660	$24.99/$37.99 CAN
Dreamweaver CS3 For Dummies	9780470114902	$24.99/$29.99 CAN
iMac For Dummies, 4th Edition	9780764584589	$21.99/$25.99 CAN
InDesign CS3 For Dummies	9780470118658	$24.99/$29.99 CAN
Macs For Dummies, 9th Edition	9780470048498	$21.99/$25.99 CAN
Photoshop CS3 All-in-One Desk Reference For Dummies	9780470111956	$39.99/$47.99 CAN
Photoshop CS3 For Dummies	9780470111932	$24.99/$29.99 CAN
PowerPoint 2007 For Dummies	9780470040591	$21.99/$25.99 CAN
Web Design For Dummies, 2nd Edition	9780471781172	$24.99/$31.99 CAN